LIVING WITH THE DEAD

Marilyn Zelke Windau

WATER'S EDGE PRESS
TUCSON, AZ

This collection of poems is a human-made work of imagination.
No part of this book may be reproduced, distributed, or transmitted
in any form or by any means without written permission of the
publisher, except in the case of brief quotations used
in a review of the book.

NO AI TRAINING: Without in any way limiting the author's
[and publisher's] exclusive rights under copyright, any use of
this publication to "train" generative artificial intelligence (AI)
technologies to generate text is expressly prohibited. The author
reserves all rights to license uses of this work for generative AI
training and development of machine learning language models.

Copyright © 2026 by Marilyn Zelke Windau

All rights reserved.

Printed in the United States of America

Water's Edge Press LLC
Tucson, AZ
watersedgepress.com

ISBN: 978-1-952526-33-6

Credits

Cover and book design by Water's Edge Press
Images licensed through VectorStock

Also by the Author

Adventures in Paradise, Finishing Line Press, 2014.
Momentary Ordinary, Pebblebrook Press, 2014.
Owning Shadows, Kelsay Books, 2017.
Hiccups Haunt Wilson Avenue, Kelsay Books, 2018.
Beneath The Southern Crux, Water's Edge Press, 2023.
Northwoods Recollections, Bottlecap Press, 2025.
Woof Worthy, Kelsay Books, 2025.

Author's Note

In 1988, when we moved into our home, our children were young. We chose the house because it has four bedrooms, a wonderful back yard in which our children could play, and ample space for gardens: flower and vegetable gardens for me to cultivate.

We knew it had once been a funeral home. We were not prepared for the degree to which the place itself would reveal its history.

People came up to us on the street and instead of giving us "welcome to the neighborhood" brownies or cookies, they would tell us scary stories. They would tell us to beware.

A former funeral director came to visit. Then a woman brought her parents all the way from Colorado. She had grown up in the house. Her parents had been employed here. Everyone had tales to tell us.

All of this became prompts for me, a poet, to write this book.

The poems in Part One are imaginary, urged on by words waking me up in the night, stories of those who may have been here, in the attic, basement, closets.

Part Two includes poems of a true nature about my family, relatives, friends—their memories and mine, and of loved ones lost to death, poems of my sorrow.

Part One

A Home 1
Process 3
In the Parlor 5
Death in the Family 7
A Special Death 8
Death of a Swan 10
Heritage 11
Slicing Time 12
Life Energy 14
Just Friends in Passing 15
Perchance to Dream 18
She Was My Teacher 19
Time Gifts Remembrance 20
Seeing Red 21
Body Identified 22
Opioid Distribution 24
Venturing Need 25
"If I Should Die" 26
Death by Speed 28
In Honor of Life 29
Hide and Seek 31
Santa's Spirits 32
Scissors Happy 34
Cause of Death 35

Part Two

Instruction 39
Jumping Ahead, Jumping Back 41
Lineage 43
Determined Spirits 44
Her Tree 45
A Familiar, Chance Encounter 46
A Message on Mother's Day 48
Gone 50
The Sixth Sense 51
Listen 53
Remains 55
Toll 57
Remembrance 59
For Instants 61
Venturing Down New Roads 62
New Age 63
Memorize Your Story 65
A Scary Discovery 66
A Dream/A Nightmare 67
Footsteps 68
Mud Story 69
Spin Cycle 70
Between Life and Death 72
Living with the Dead 73
The Secret 75

Part One

A Home

There are five doors on the ground floor.
This house had many openings for life
and for honoring those departed.

I live in a former funeral home.
Why it's called a home, I don't know.
Who is housed here?

There are many spirits,
Many souls who have departed
through the confines of these rooms,
these walls, these portals.

We came here as a family of five
twenty-one years after the closing
of these death's doors to the community.

Yet, our new neighbors did not bring
brownies, welcome cookies,
pots of flowers.

Passersby did warn my youngsters
not to dig in the back gardens,
not to open the attic door at night—
for spirits lurked, they said.

For many years the spirits have been friendly—
noisy, at times,
with their squeaks and thumps.
Who would deny them their music?
Sometimes it's easy to tell the men
from the women, the aged from the young.

There's a softness in between the clamor,
a reality in between the dream,
a distance in between the grave,
a yearning in between the grounding.

Process

The stairs to the cellar creak.
They moan the weight of bodies brought down.
Three times a week or twice a day, no matter: death occurs.

Someone has to take charge of death.
This house was the one for our community.

Big and stately, erected in 1891,
it bore character and memories.
A family home for many years,
it became a furniture store in the 1920's.
Room groupings were a novel idea then—
and the store could offer you
your final piece of furniture, a coffin.

Death, being more lucrative than bedroom sets,
gave impetus for the house to become a funeral home.
Now, its prominence could be celebrated
in life and in the hereafter.

Three cisterns were built in the basement.
Rainwater washed insects, bird droppings,
dead creatures down the roof to gutters,
to downspouts, and finally to cisterns.
Neighbors cleaned out each other's cisterns.
That way owners never knew
the horrible contents of their own.

Cistern water was used to wash the dead,
to keep the bodies cool
until embalming could be done,
hair coiffed, face make up applied,
arms positioned just so.

Flesh was preservered in a satin-lined coffin,
displayed in the front parlor,
or in the upstairs viewing room with Ionic columns
and brocade curtains,
the room where I now restfully sleep nightly.

In the Parlor

They never asked the cause.
An unmarked car just drove
into their circular driveway.
Black, long, with passengers:
one living, one dead.

The appointment had been made earlier,
after the fact, after the breathing had stopped,
after the heart had ceased to beat.

The family wanted a simple coffin,
shoes: her favorite black pumps,
and black lace underwear—
no one would see that—
a tailored suit, plaid serge,
her hair done in a bob.
All was arranged as requested.

Her hands were placed atop her abdomen,
one over the other,
but three inches above her body,
and two inches between each other.
In time, touching meant early breakage.

The staff stood by at the service
smiling solemnly, greeting unknown relatives,
the clients with downcast eyes,
solicitous gestures.

Twice during the year,
the funeral home offered remembrance gatherings,
guidance hours, sympathy sessions.
These were well attended at holiday times.

Their parlor was always busy.
They could count on death annually.
Even in poor times,
death outlived taxes.

Death in the Family

Who bought you that little blue suit
to lie down in,
hemmed those pants six and a half inches up?
You, who'd not known dresswear ever,
who'd only known torn knees, ripped sleeves,
scuffed shoes, dirtied socks.
Too little, too young.
Unknowing, unready.
We will take care of all.
We provide, sustain,
withstand, undertake.

A Special Death

We were down at the quarry lake.
Most of the town's people were there.
A cold December day,
but skaters took to the thin ice anyway.

I lost hold of his hand.
I kept hold of his mitten,
a four-year old's blue mitten.

I searched and shouted my son's name.
He didn't say, "Hey, mom,
Look at me! Here I am!"

He, in snow pants,
those leg weights,
descended the cold
when he broke through.

They said my baby's funeral
was the saddest one ever held
at the funeral parlor.

They built a special coffin for him,
crowned it with a little carved bear.
He always loved fuzzy bears.

My husband blamed me.
I lost his son.
He sought divorce,
as though I hadn't lost enough.

Crying and prayer cards,
pale lips and cold skin,
repeated words of condolences,
of sympathy, of regret.
Whose fault is death?
Whose responsibility is life?

Death of a Swan

They dressed her in pink taffeta.
She had always loved the sound it made
when she scrunched it in her hands
before ballet recitals.

She never gained acclaim as a dancer.
Instead, she ran a hamburger haven
outside Muskego, Wisconsin,
with her husband, who weekly beat her
though she was not to blame.

She continued to dream of *Swan Lake*,
the bowing and fluttering of her wings,
her adult life earthbound
except for her imagination.

Pink sheets, pink pillowcases,
pink bedspreads, pink hyacinths
were the memories she held dear.

She rests now, in intermission,
before the final act when she will glide
on those toe shoes *en pointe* to heaven,
and cover her head with the wings of angels.

Heritage

She had raised five children for him.
He was out in fields from sunrise on.
The boys and girls were healthy and strong,
schooled and sheltered on the farm.
More and more and more was the want:
children subscripted to the plow, to the seeding,
the weeding, the harvest.

When was their dream time?
Where was their hope?

She knew they wanted life.
She knew she was not the one to cede it.

When their father died,
being kicked in the head by an obedient cow,
she saw the joy,
as well as the remorse, on their faces.

They left her, as they should,
but returned often,
to clasp her hand, hug her shoulder,
kiss her cheek, glance at their father's portrait.

Strength is inherited,
from one line or another.

Slicing Time

You know, I thought about slicing them—
those people who always come in asking for a deal.
They're cheapskates.
I'm a butcher!
I hack apart animals.
I reek of blood.
I have sinew under my fingernails.
I leave no bone unturned.
I leave much of the fat on.
When you charge by the pound,
you have to count the fat.
Profits are the wished for.

I wish for funds!
My son needs glasses.
My daughter needs a winter coat.
My wife wants new carpeting.
My doctor says I'm dying.
My insurance gives them what they all need,
but what of me?

I want to live!
I don't want to be a dead contributor.

The hanging steers in the cooler
laugh at me.
The little lambs weep.
The chickens cackle every day.
The turkeys gobble their grief yearly.

Life is a slice of time.
Some get a thick chop.
I get a thin filet.
Some lives are ground meat.
Some lives are prime.
As a butcher, I am in control of the depth of life.
As a man, I am in control of nothing.
Whichever way I slice it,
I have to punch the time clock out.

Life Energy

She and her sister played
around the roots of this big tree,
this tree that their mother
examined daily in spring,
waiting to joyfully announce,
"Leaves are budding!"

When their mother died,
they revisited the big tree.
It had grown on the family farm
for a hundred years or more.

The sisters now made a pact.
They would share their bodies' dust together.
Their ashes would come home, remain home.
They would nurture tree and earth at death.

A storm blew that all asunder.
Lightning split the tree in half
decimating their wish.

Down and fallen,
the oak awaits an acorn,
a seed for new growth
to be nurtured to new life.

The sisters wait, with energy to give.

Just Friends in Passing

She woke up.
It was very dark in her room.
Pulling the curtain just a few inches,
she could see no stars out her window.
She was thirsty, wanted the glass of water
her mother had placed on her desk at bedtime.

"I'll get it for you," said a quiet voice.

"What? Who are you? Where are you?
What are you doing in my room?
How do you know what I want?" the girl asked.

"It's me, Melody!
This used to be my room a long, long time ago.
I had two brothers and a sister.
We had a cat named Purrfect.
She used to sleep on my bed with me.
She knew when I had a bad dream
and would nuzzle my nose."

"We have a dog, Goldie.
He always wants to come up on my bed,
but my mom shoos him off.
She says he might have fleas.
I think she just doesn't want
more wash to do."

"What's your name?
I saw you move in last month.
Did you get to pick my room?"

"I loved this room when I saw it.

I didn't know it was your room.
My name is Merry.
When we first got here
the neighbors made me afraid.
They said not to dig in the garden
and not to sleep by the attic stairs.
They said the house was haunted
and that I should beware."

"Oh, you don't have to worry.
I'm not mean and scary.
I'm just Melody.
You don't have to be afraid.
I'd like to be your friend.
Do you like to play with dolls?
I have one in the attic that I hid
so my brothers wouldn't pull her arms off.
My brothers were horrible.
They're not here anymore though.
They got to grow up and get married.
My sister, too.
I didn't.
I just lived here 'til I was nine.
I got real sick.
I think they called it 'red fever.'"

"I had a temperature once.
My mom gave me water.
She always leaves a glass on my desk
so that if I wake up, I can drink it.
Do you want some, Melody?"

"Oh, no, Merry!
It's of no use to me now, but thank you!"

"How come I can't see you, only hear you?"

"It's because I am like a dream to you—
not a nightmare!
Someday, after we are really, truly friends
I think you will see me, as I see you.
I hope so, because I'd really like that."

"I'd like that, too, Melody.
Now I have to go back to sleep."

"Me, too, Merry,
even though I have been sleeping for such a long time,
waiting for a friend."

Perchance to Dream

He said, "I'm going to go to sleep now.
Don't try to wake me. I'm going to sleep for a long time.
I hope to dream."

His last words before passing defined death for me.
Sleep is such a comfort, a time for stories,
for visions, for being introduced to the unknown
with no fear, just an excitement of discovery.

My church upbringing told me
that He has a house with many rooms,
plenty of space to let me explore,
to reunite, to endure this next phase
which is not infanthood—or is it?

There are those who believe in rebirth
to work out issues of the past life,
to gain understanding, to progress.
That in mind, I delve now into playing
with my grandchildren, into finishing tasks,
eliminating items from the next life's to do list.

I myself have a house of many rooms.
I'm hoping that I will be able to sleep tonight—
perchance to dream,
and awaken to a new day of possibilities.

She Was My Teacher

They came in throngs to this house
to see their teacher for the last time.
Children led their parents,
pulling them by their hands forward.

"Commemorate" is a big word,
 a word many fourth graders would stumble on.
These children had lately learned its meaning.

This was their teacher—
she, who said good morning to them every day,
she, who asked them to rise from their seats,
to say the Pledge of Allegiance.

They cried now.
They hung their heads.
Who can understand death
at such an early age?

Absence is keen.
Memory is treasure.
Names and faces stay.

Time Gifts Remembrance

I wanted to tell Santa to make me well.
I wanted to tell Santa to make my mom smile.
I wanted my dad to give me a hug.
He wasn't a hugger, but he loved me.

I went to kindergarten.
I met lots of kids my own age.
We had fun at recess playing tag.
I was a little slower than most of the boys.
They didn't make a big deal out of it.

Santa came for seven years to my house.
He might have come after that for my sister.
I don't know because I wasn't there.

My baby sister was really cute.
She had dark hair, curly.
Her eyes were sometimes green
and sometimes brown.
It was weird, but pretty.

I feel bad that I didn't get to know her.
How can you get to know someone
when you're not alive?

My dad would say, "What a roll of the dice!"

He thinks now about that.
He's eighty-three.
My sister is forty-five, has four children.
Time, as they say, marches on.
I would prefer that they say,
"Time gifts remembrance."

Seeing Red

Everything was a blur.
The drops she put in my eyes
shed yellow tears into the tissue.
I stared at the far chart,
could only see the big D.
Then I heard it—the crash,
the mayhem that followed:
shouting, doors opening,
slamming shut, feet running.
I got up, turned my room's lock,
sat back, sank my head into the
cushioned chair and waited.

A patient in the next room
had had a heart attack, died,
after asking the doctor
what it was he had seen
when she shined the bright light.
"It's your blood vessels.
They look like rivers of red
flowing through a desert."

She thought he had fainted,
didn't know of his blood phobia.
The EMT quietly shut his dilated eyes.

Body Identified

It was raining, hard!
He ran out to find his pup.
Paddling fast, the dog made it.
His boyhood friend drowned.
The stream flooded its banks
with tears.

She was a dancer, an actor.
Her smile curved her face,
as her movements curved the floor.
A student of life's gestures
was caught short in Texas.
The world's stage is dark this night.

Pending notification of family
a young man was shot, killed
out front of a house on the north side.
He was delivering pizza.
His wife and children waited,
couldn't understand how
just going to work gets you dead.

She was cuddling with her granddad.
He was reading her a bedtime story.
Three years old, a bullet penetrated
the house, penetrated her.
The "once upon a time" story
ended time for her.
Not happily ever after, but
a grim tale of neighborhood violence
gone awry.

So many nightly news accounts
reveal bodies identified,
as if the story ends there.
For many of us, the story begins there.
We, who take notice,
having been notified daily
of these newsworthy occurrences,
feel pain at adding another of us to the list
of humans gone too soon, unjustified, identified
solely as numbers to be added.

Opioid Distribution

Over by the downtown park,
an elderly woman opens her door
at a bell ring.

A young man waits there, impatiently.
He is tall, skinny, about twenty years old,
the same age as one of her grandchildren.
He shifts his weight from one foot to the other,
holds out his hand.

She nods, passes a brown paper bag to him.
He looks inside,
like it's his middle school lunch sack.

Digging into his pocket, he withdraws
a wad of bills—twenties, hands them to her.
She accepts them, smiling,
not knowing the deaths she has created.

Tim's short life will be celebrated today
in the front parlor.
The elderly woman will rest here next year
before burial.

Venturing Need

You went out, Mom.
We were in our beds
as you told us to be.
We heard a noise.
Clare came in my room.
She was afraid.
She made me afraid.
We hid under my bed, Mom.
There was a man.
He was loud.
He found us mom.
He dragged us out.
He wanted money.
We gave him our allowances.
It wasn't enough.
He hit Clare.
I hit him.
Where were you, Mom,
when we died?

"If I Should Die"

She had said it every night
since she was a small girl,
having learned it at church:
"Now I lay me down to sleep,
I pray the Lord my soul to keep.
If I should die before I wake,
I pray the Lord my soul to take."

She pulled over her head a flannel gown,
a favorite, given to her for Christmas
from her eldest granddaughter.
It was white with red and blue flowers,
trailing bright green leaves.

She had been cold in the front parlor,
had gone upstairs to get ready for bed.
It was the bed she had first shared
with her husband, gone these seven years.

They had created four children there,
three still living, one gone at age three
from scarlet fever.

Amazing, the accomplishments of time!
One son a doctor, one daughter a lawyer,
the youngest an artist with works hanging
in celebrated galleries.

Grandchildren with smiles, some toothless,
some grinning across their faces.
They were a joy not anticipated.

She looked forward to the days
of making cookies with them—
all kinds: chocolate chip, soft molasses,
rice crispy treats, sugar cookies shaped in hearts.
They were her future.

She climbed into the soft bed,
pulled the covers up to her chin,
turned to her left shoulder,
eased the pillow to hold her face.

She counted, as she had for years,
backwards from eighty-nine,
breathing in and out while counting.
It helped, as it always had,
especially when she visualized water—
the ocean calm, the ocean in waves,
the ocean blue green.

The artist son found her,
smiling that small smile,
cozy in comfort,
her soul kept safely.

Death by Speed

He flew past me going seventy
in a 35-mph zone.
Since the governor gave credence
to speed, he thought he was entitled.
What he didn't know was that
at the merge right
there was an ice slick.
Fire in a roadside house
had brought the squad.
Cold temperatures freeze water,
water which saves, ice which doesn't.
He lies here now in the front parlor,
hands clasped, immobile.
The smile on his face reads false.
Is heaven a race track?

In Honor of Life

I was making a living.
I was making a life.
I had asked for her hand.
Her parents were willing.
Her father saw himself in me:
the labor, the work hours,
the tenacity, the strength
of mind over muscle,
of dream over reality.

Our wedding was planned:
the church, the minister,
the ceremony, the words of union,
the exchange of rings: I do and I will.

My mother's ring I would wind on her finger—
she, who was no longer with me, with us,
from my eighth year.
I requested syllabub in her honor at our party.
My boisterous friends would do us honor
and raucously chide me for my lust.

There on the dance floor,
my new wife twirled me.
I suddenly sank to my knees, to my chest,
felt pain equal to my love for her,
felt distance, long sight distance,
as if looking over our corn fields,
as if watching our border collie
gather the sheep from afar.

I heard shouts and weeping.
I saw her future alone.
I saw infinity creeping
from my ankles to my calves,
to my loins, which would never father children.

Is it enough that I follow her,
even now?
Is it enough that I love her,
even now?
Is it enough that she makes a life
which we should have made together,
that she honors, even now.

Hide and Seek

We used to play hide and seek.
I still do, even thought my sisters
and brothers are gone.
They grew up!
I was left here, in the old house,
the funeral parlor, to play by myself.

How do you play hide and seek by yourself?

I waited! That was the answer!
Voices called to me in the dark—
young voices, wanting.

Finally, after a long time
a little girl moved into my house.
She was pretty, with dark hair.

I tried to talk to her in her dreams.
She rolled over and snored.

I tried to talk to her in the day.
She told me to "bug off!"

Not being a bug,
Not knowing what I am now,
I hesitated trying to communicate.

There was a young lad who died
at about the same time as I did.
We became good friends and stopped
trying to please the girl.

Santa's Spirits

The best thing about being in the spirit world—
that time and space when your physical self
is absent of them—
is Christmas.

Children all over the world wait and hope,
write letters to the North Pole, see and talk
to elves in their dreams.
They are on their best behavior for weeks,
ever wishing for their wishes to come true.

We, who die young, have an advantage over Santa.
He is one of us, though older.
He wears bright colors and fluff on his hat,
on his boots.
His mother must have picked out his wardrobe!

We can see that the twinkle in his eye
is one that we had as well.
It's an eye-bob that a parent cannot decipher.
It's a sneaky glance, a quiet nod with eyes turned up,
cast almost to heaven.

He might hear you when you're sleeping.
He might know when you're awake.
We spirit children hear him, know where he is.
We know that he is good, not bad,
and we are incapable of being otherwise.

We wait for him December 24th every year.
We share the cookies, hug the reindeer,
jingle the bells on his sleigh.
His presence is our presents.

We are spirits who link repeatedly,
year after year—
spirits who join travels in chimneys, in vast skies:
world journeys.

We spirits can go there every day,
but the most special day is a night:
Christmas Eve.

Scissors Happy

Martha looked longingly from her bed
at the pile of fabric wedged
against her sewing machine.
It was an old model, a treadle Singer.
She'd sewn on it for seventy years,
since she was taught as a girl of twelve.

The rhythm of her long, narrow foot
had made music—a dance
of color, of pattern.
She had composed shirts and skirts
and curtains, ties and dresses and quilts.

Squares of cloth now bombarded her dreams.
She created mind designs at midnight
which awakened her at three.

Seeking scissors was her mission.
Swinging her legs out of bed was easy.
Standing and walking was not possible.
A thump and a clunk brought her niece.

She found her aged aunt on the floor,
reaching for the cotton, the fabric of a last quilt—
a quilt that she would now finish in Martha's honor.

Cause of Death

The newspaper never tells us.
The church bulletin never tells us.
Those just list name, age,
schooling, marriage, children,
grandchildren, great grandchildren,
employment, and the site
for providing comfort at the last event.

Is it too personal to name
the reason for death?
Is it more personal than a wife's name,
husband's name, children's names?

Heart disease, stroke, food poisoning
caused by recalled romaine lettuce,
black beans at the Mexican restaurant,
Alzheimer's with pneumonia,
diabetic shock, tooth decay?

Your history is our history
in a small town.
We all yield to the summons
of a funeral at the big house.

There, hidden voices whisper
in the upstairs viewing room
and in the downstairs parlor.

Those to reach the casket first
with a firm hand hold,
with a smile, a shoulder hug,

a downward, pious eye
await the cause of death,
valuing the knowledge
as privileged information.

Service done, they leave early,
impart their learning to neighbors,
reining in the kudos of the untold,
those of less advantage.

Part Two

Instruction

> *"One of the last things you should teach your children is how to die."*
> —Kevin Toolis, *"My Father's Wake"*

I sat with my dead father,
like Marley his chin bandaged up round his head.
I realized that the bandage kept his mouth closed.
It wasn't often.

We tend to droop, when we relax into death.
It may be that death is a comfort,
after such a struggle to remain in the physical world.
Pneumonia took him, with an Alzheimer's lead in.

My brother, just a year and a month younger than me,
found death as a surprise.
"It's flu. It's nothing. I'll be fine.
No, I don't want to see a doctor.
Be still, my heart."
"Yes," it answered.

I sat with my mother, humming classical music
of Beethoven, telling her it was okay to let go.
What did I know of death to be telling her?
She fingered the photograph of my father,
seeking his unity in silent quest.

Still, I protested, summoned nurses,
calling her name, "Mom!"
"She's gone," they said.

Where is it that we go at death?
There's no GPS to locate our coordinates.
Some, of faith, think there is an otherworldly place
with gates and gardens and forever.

I question the gates, the captivity.

Gardens are ongoing in their summons of life.
I can teach my children that to die is to plant,
to regenerate generations,
to gather from the soil of DNA
those attributes which are unique,
yet echo in the worthy lives of ancestry.
For ancestry is not stagnant.
It is a continuum of growth
from seed, to bud, to blossom, to fruition,
and remembrance.

Jumping Ahead, Jumping Back

I read the last page of the book.
I know. I shouldn't have done it.
I wish I'd read your life story sooner.
Your childhood pictures,
your elementary school grade cards,
with pluses and A's,
your scouting days of writing,
published in the *Nature Tribe*
as a Lone Scout at eleven years old.

And so many pictures of Alice,
your friend from grade school 'til when?
She wasn't my mom.
Mom was much later.
You met her after the "wreck,"
when your brother crashed the car,
when they declared you critical,
cannot survive.

You did though and graduated with honors
to become a professor of journalism,
a speech writer for a congressman,
a skate dancer, an ad man,
an editor, a husband, a father.

I read your story now.
I'm sixty-eight. You wouldn't believe it,
still tall, skinny as a rail.
You've been gone since 1990.
Too late to ask you the names
or the faces in your scrapbooks.

I post to scouting archives, to historical societies,
to progressive newspapers, to fraternity,
to departments of agriculture—
all those papers of memorabilia
of your life lived.

I read the last page of your book of life.
I just wish I had talked more with you, the author.
I understand now, after your death,
the importance sought by a life.

Lineage

No wonder you gravitated to your mom.
Your dad was a rabble rouser, like your older brother.
Your dad gave him his own childhood nickname: Pinkie.
Who knows where that came from? Complexion?
Last little genetic finger with a bend?

I never knew if you had a nickname.
It's tough being second born.
I understand. I'm one, too.

You cried at your mom's visitation.
You were behind a curtain with my mother.
I was five years old.
I remember that sobbing.
I knew it was you. I knew that depth, even at my age.
I still remember, though I don't remember
much about my Gramma Mamie.

I can see the big wooden doll house in her back yard,
the garden overwhelmed with raspberries.
I can see you spooning raspberries over
vanilla ice cream, scooped into a "mush" melon.

Ray, my only brother, had that finger, too,
just like Marlyn, your brother.
He didn't acquire the nickname of Pinkie.
He acquired "Butch,"
the nickname of your brother's adopted son.

I was given the female variation of your brother's name.

When do we stop trying to please?
When does second stop being not good enough?

Determined Spirits

She had survived the depression years,
helping on the farm as best she could.
Her father had died. Her mother was careworn,
digging potatoes to gain five cents a bushel.

She, the youngest child, remembered her father
scaring "the living daylights"
out of her and school chums
when he sprang from behind fences
as they passed her farm's borders
on their walk home from school.

She lived to marry, bear three children,
work as a teacher until age eighty-three.
She kept her husband safe until she couldn't.
Dementia lingered until pneumonia caught him.

Now they both quietly traverse stairs from the attic,
each with individual purpose.
She needs to check that the stove is off,
the iron unplugged, the doors locked.
He needs to go to the mailbox to see
if a *US News and World Report*
has been delivered this day.
Fallout shelter designs they post
instill a need to protect his family.

In the night they retreat to the attic,
stare at the star-filled sky,
remember the past, and the future.

Her Tree

I pull it out gently from its 4 x 4 x 40-inch box.
It has a wooden cube base, painted beige
with a garland decoration.
Its limbs are iffy.
They are taped now to the trunk,
a solid pole with an aluminum star atop.

It's her tree from when she was a five-year-old girl
awaiting Santa and small gifts in 1918 in Muskego.
She didn't know her brother would die
upstairs in his room that year.
He hadn't gone to the war.
He was the only son on the farm, and thus exempt.

Instead, the war came to him
with sickened schoolmates sent back ill
from France, home of the pigs kept for soldiers' food,
home of the pigs infected with swine flu.

She heard him cry and rail in his bed at the top of the stairs.
She decorated the little tree in his honor and in hope.
She slept downstairs on a small bench in the big room,
near the heat register, curled up with a blanket,
to wait for a Christmas miracle.

The tree survived.
I decorate it now with little ornaments,
remembering a hundred years of wishes,
and my own longing for my brother,
gone these several years past.

A Familiar, Chance Encounter

She was looking forward.
I was looking back.
A girl wearing glasses
followed my car,
unaware that she was driving your car.

I was in Sheboygan, on my way home.
There it was: your turquoise blue
Honda hatchback,
the one I had to sell in Wisconsin
to settle your estate in Illinois.

A new owner, she was a good driver,
kept a distance, signaled her turn
into the Piggly Wiggly parking lot.
You always did like to go grocery shopping.
You'd check the ad sheets,
then aim for the best deal,
sometimes wheeling and dealing
to three stores, smacking a high five
on the roof of your car.

I kept returning to the rear view—
the mirror in which I hoped to see you,
my brother, gone these many years.
She didn't let on that she knew—
knew I was staring, knew it was his car,
that I wished to see a different driver.

Each time I spot your car,
it's become a comfort—
my quick glimpse of the rusted back left fender,
a flash of blue, low to the ground,
the jolt of first gear to second
manually sticking that shift,
the little dent in the front hood
where your anger erupted, your fist pounded
when Dad died.

It's become a comfort
to know that something of you
is left to encounter,
a surprise of familiarity
if only by chance.

A Message on Mother's Day

Sometimes I wake up in the night.
Usually it's because of your breathing,
your snoring, your kick-leg thrust.

Last night, it wasn't about you.
It was about my sister.
She sent a card to me—
a Mother's Day card.

It wasn't for me.
It was for our mother,
who has been dead for nine years.

She wanted me to send the card to Mom.
She is thick into dementia,
genetically gifted from our father.

It's a nice card.
Mom loved sending cards for all occasions.
If one card was good, three were better!
My sister remembers a few things.
She knows a card is meaningful.

I will place the card in a plastic zip bag.
I will take it to the cemetery.
I will dig for it a shallow safety deposit box.

Your love will be guarded there,
in her earth place.
She will know, even though she always knew,
that you, her first-born, were special.

She will remember, fondly,
your baby curls, your daffodil party
at age five, your ballerina recital *en pointe*,
your mastering Brahms at piano lessons,
your role as Wendy in drama class
downtown for Peter Pan.

She will feel your presence,
know your longing,
want the hug which is always there.

Gone

Who do I know that's an extra-large men's?
I bought you a blue shirt for Christmas.
I was going to wrap it after I made cookies,
so I could include them in the gift I would mail
to the nursing home for you and my sister.

You would have liked them, as you liked
the Snickers and fudge we brought you in October—
the day we visited you.
You had a sweet tooth.

I talked to my sister in the dining room then for minutes.
She twisted a bit of napkin around and around
her left-hand index finger.
Neither of us noticed that another woman at our table
took the plastic container of tartar sauce
from your tray, opened it, was licking it.

Neither of us noticed that you were in the hallway
talking with my husband, who told me later that
you had asked him for money.
Given a twenty, you said,
"Can I have $5 more?"

Now, a few weeks after making you smile,
you are dead. You tried to make it to ninety, but failed.

Do we ever have control?
Will she notice you are gone?
Will she miss someone calling her Sweetie?

The Sixth Sense

In that movie, years ago, there was a child
who could see the dead. It plagued him,
frightened, and enlightened him.

I have the same offering,
though, I knew many of the dead.

They speak from airspace, from envelopes
with stamps placed upside down,
perhaps in protest, perhaps in fun
in 1931 and 1918 and all those years
before I became.

I relive my relatives' lives
in posted letters, time-colored,
toasted almond by years.

They impart a reflection,
a small focused view
of a town, a time, lives of the living.

Gossip and meal menus,
health worries and funerals,
of everyone down the block,
all at church, the neighbors,
smashed, not mashed potatoes,
birds at the feeder this day,
this week, this year.

All are chronicled.
All are worthy of remembrance,
of imparting love in messages,
to those away from home,
so that they, in turn, though absent,
can commune.

I am one.
My children wrote letters home from camp.
I saved them.
I save these from my mother as well
for we share a sixth sense.

Listen

"She can hear you.
Keep talking to her," the hospice nurse said.
"Hearing is the last of the senses to leave."

I didn't know the rules of dying.
I didn't know the mottling of feet,
that the closed eyes were rest, not death.

I played tapes of Mozart,
of Debussy, Beethoven, Ravel—
background music in a nursing home
which tuned its radio to Kenny Chesney
at the nurses' station.

My mother seemed to quiet to the classics.
I hoped they were right,
that she heard those comforting chords
of the masters she had played on the piano
at her church, her college programs,
at home with me and my siblings huddled
in the living room, listening beneath the baby grand,
bought secondhand.

Now, years later, my first grandchild is born.
I watch this infant fall asleep
to my humming, to my singing, and rocking.

His mother imparts to me
what natal nurses told her—
that hearing is the first sense,
the strongest sense which life brings.

A baby cries,
hears its own voice,
claims position,
a place in the world.

Life gives us an auditory gift
to welcome us, to encourage us,
to urge us onward at our beginning,
to soothe and sustain us later, finally.

Remains

I read them, more often than not.
Never more than two-inch columns long
and never more than two inches wide.
They never relate cause of death,
state only birth, and age,
relatives and work history,
time and date of service,
donations can be sent to www.

What a way to go,
buried at the bottom of page seven
of the local small-town newspaper.

Please, send me off with a poem
of hope, or at least give my audience
a reason why I passed from this life
at this age, in this year.

It was pneumonia.
It was a heart attack.
I was run over by someone
speeding down the main highway,
the gateway to our fair city.
It was death by gas.

My last words were quoted as
"Would that I had taken Silver Sneakers
Meditation classes more seriously."
"Valentine's Day is a failure."
"Speed limit is 25 mph here!"
"Farting is overrated."

Let people know where they can come to visit me.
Give them my books' references,
my children's phone numbers,
maps to garden plots I tended in life.
Give them my leftover Piggly Wiggly
cents-off coupons for gasoline.

Allow them to sift through my memorabilia,
and that of my parents, grandparents—
the history of an extended family
settled, rooted, solid as stone
in this state, once physical,
now spiritual, of Wisconsin.
I won't ever leave here.
I will remain.

Toll

"Ask not for whom the bell tolls. It tolls for thee." John Donne

A strange word: toll.
There is a singing in it, a melody of peal.
It rings a circle of sound, advances forward,
insistent as future to the ear.

Charon charges a toll.
He extracts it from your mouth,
where living relatives place it in hope.
Because of it, you can be transported
across the river Styx from the realm of the living
to your next home with the welcoming dead.

No coin? No boat ride.
You are doomed to wander the earth,
where no one can see you, hear your voice,
feel your wrinkled skin, smell the odors you exude.

Expressways take their toll as well.
With an I Pass you zoom
under a camera at seventy miles an hour,
never realizing that your toll has been paid.

You don't need a coin under your tongue,
or coins in your pocket.
Charon, of the Pennsylvania Turnpike,
smiles as you cross over, is instantly compensated.

Life claims its toll, silently.
You watch as your parents, siblings become infirm, die.
You see your children birth children
and you wonder at your age, wanting,
always wanting, more time.

Where can I pay?
Is there an installment plan?
How many points have I earned
this month on my life toll credit card?
Is my Styx crossing free?
Is there a rebate for rebirth?

Remembrance

A crooked pinkie finger?
A Rh-negative factor?
Two toes linked on one tendon?

An introvert tendency to write,
to hide out in the dry bathtub,
to play music by ear?

A predisposition for saltwater taffy?
A fear of belly button security?
An innate sense of worldly community?

A love for sorting, for grouping and analyzing,
for decision making,
for interpreting value on a personal scale?

For responsibility at a young age,
for mindful closure of asked-for duties,
for repentance of those not yet accomplished,
decades later?

Generations ask their progeny for answers,
sensing that they do not have more time.

Children do not always know the questions.
They want to help but find that possibilities
come in overflowing baskets,
in reams of text, in tubs of memorabilia,
in remembered requests.

Listen, and own your own life
as I own my own life.

My wish for my children is that they own theirs.
My wish for my children's children is that they glory
in the history, the loves, the peculiarities
of those of their bonding that have gone before.

Listen.
These are the stories that are meant to be told.
These are the oral traditions of family to be treasured.

For Instants

A cool burst of air hits my summer perspiring arm,
turns hairs into amber wheat sheaves shifting.
A bell chimes in a church tower two blocks away,
sounds a beckon of invitation.
Mown grass—epee blades—lie tilted
on the still growing green.
An open-top truck, mounded with potatoes,
wheels my street seeking the expressway.
A day's instants, once perceived.

Today, in Nya Trang, on a temple bench
a woman sits in the shade of Buddhist statuary.
She looks down corridors of tombs,
ashes of ancestors held fast in wall cells.
Above her, wind murmurs bamboo leaves,
flicks sun silver over her black hair,
glints light on her few of white.

I don't see her face.
I don't know her name.
I don't speak her language.
Yet, in an instant,
she becomes a part of my life,
a part of my history,
forever encapsulated
in the maze of cells that is my brain.

Venturing Down New Roads

Roads of crinkled flesh,
thighs that hang skin,
face that gives roads south from lips.
I can see the ages, though I don't feel
the ages of chronological time.
Is this me?

Sometimes I am a mind without a body.
Asian beetles and box elder bugs join me
in my winter of discontent.
I follow their days, talk to them.
They are content to traverse my hand,
my bathroom window, to seek moisture
and sustenance this winter.

I breathe in, breathe out
yoga exercises.
I calm my aged mind for minutes.

There is a downward dog in my kitchen.
She wants breakfast.
She knows the words, "Eat slowly."
She waits for those words.

Is there another measure of time?
Can I please be a part of that?
Who is it that can grant me my wish?

I believe it is within me to gift
treasures of thought, of meaning,
of life.

Amen means let it be so.
Amen then.

New Age

Corduroy roads of thump thump skinny pines.
Break your back crank engine automobiles.
Swivel twisted ear pieces on mounted telephones
your great-great-grandad hit his bald pate on
when rising from his chair.
Live neighbor women's voices to direct your calls.
Lard and honey on whole wheat toast.
Skating the river to a one room schoolhouse.
Lone Scouts.

Digit dialed telephones
with nouns to remember:
Palisades, Pensacola, Central...
as well as numbers.
Keys for locks.
Mail in the post box,
milk in the milk box,
coal down the cellar chute.
student standby flights.
Power steering.
A man on the moon!
A president shot, killed
not in Roy Rogers style,
Maverick's, or Marshall Dillon's.
Not by the good guys.

Oh, Grandma! Tell me more stories.
No cell phones, no computers,
no internet, no space stations,
no microwave popcorn,
no cable TV.

This new age ages you
just as it did me.
Oh, the stories you'll tell!
Your children await.

Memorize Your Story

I saw the big advertising sign as I passed
the cemetery, the mausoleum.
It made me think about my parents,
my brother, my ancestors,
all who wait to have their story told.

Being a poet gives me permission
to tell stories, tales of the past,
anecdotes of youth and age,
trouble and mirth,
school accomplishments,
baby fun and toddler mischief,
junior high jaunts,
job hunts, adult travails,
elder musings.

It all comes down to the essence,
life being a tale,
a story to be shared.

Many are never written.
Oh, what an absence of joy!

Children grow up on stories—
why not the stories of family
who came before?
Stories of ships from Scotland,
of farms in Wisconsin.
Stories of dancing in the White House,
of mentoring an astronaut.
Stories of digging potatoes for five cents a bushel,
of diving for clam shells to pay to go to college.

1,001 nights might not be enough.

A Scary Discovery

Our garage is huge.
It used to house horses
and carriages and hay.
There are two little doors
at the rear of the garage
which open to the crawlspace.

My sisters and some of our friends
decided one warm day
to explore.

We crawled in, one after the other.
The dirt floor was powdery,
covered our pants with dust.

There in that dirt, we found it:
an eye patch, a black eye patch!
Whose was it, we wondered.

A pirate's? A murderer's?
A ghost's?
Where is the body?

We scrambled out of there
as fast as we could.

The eye patch disappeared
after we gave it to Mom.
We hope she threw it away!
The memory of it stayed.

A Dream/A Nightmare

With wide open eyes,
I sat bolt upright in my bed.
A greyish-white figure
with a human-like body
sat there at the edge.

Its strange ghostly face stared at me.
From out of its mouth poured
round metal washers—
hundreds of them.
They clunked to the carpeted floor
silently.

It didn't speak, just eyed me.
It never blinked.

I tried to scream, to make noise
but no sound exited my mouth.

I ran to my parents' room to escape.
In horror, I told my middle school friends
my dream/my nightmare later that morning.

Footsteps

Mom was in the kitchen.
My sisters and I brought plates,
silverware, glasses from the dining room.
Back again we went to clear the table
of platters and bowls, salt and pepper shakers.

Warm water filled the sink with bubbles
as Dad squirted detergent from afar
in a long arc, just barely missing Mom.

Our dog, Sandy, raised her nose,
hopeful for any leftover bits of dinner.

Suddenly, she stopped, looked upward
toward the stairway.

As if in unison, we all stopped as well!

Footsteps! We heard footsteps upstairs.

"Someone's up there," Mom whispered.
"I heard it too!"
"Me, too!"
"Me, too!"

Scared, we hugged and huddled together.

Dad, braver than any of us, ventured up.
We heard his footsteps also, but now, no others.

We remain puzzled to this day.

Mud Story

The beets, carrots, spinach, and I
couldn't wait to spoon-handle
tunnel ourselves into clumpy garden mud.
On the fourth row of subway paths,
I uncovered an old hinge.

Moisture-aged and rusty shut,
how long had it been there?
Had it come from the stable door,
the door that had to swing open to allow
horses to get in and out.

Had a brown and white horse named Pudding
nosed it, hoof-turned it
while waiting anxiously for dinner hay?

Had the owner's little boy played
in secret with his father's tools,
then pitched the hinge when spotted?

Mud can reveal stories,
a century's worth of history,
in a garden next to a garage,
which was once a stable
and a carriage house in 1891.

Spin Cycle

It was a huge load
she carried down the stairs
from the second floor.
Opening the door to the cellar,
she switched the weight
of the laundry basket
to her left hip.

The usual musty smell of damp,
of cracked concrete, of old house
pervaded her nostrils.

She set the overflowing container
onto the floor,
proceeded to align color
with color, white with white.

As she sorted, she felt strange:
a feeling, a sense of someone,
something watching her.

She loaded the darks
into the washer,
turned the dial to warm,
regular.

She didn't feel warm
or regular.
Cold and delicate
was more like it.

She had often had this feeling
in the 1891 house—
that those of old were here,
but here to guide her.
They had always befriended,
supported, comforted her.

This was different.
This was threatening.

She put the cover on the liquid soap,
closed the lid of the washer.
The familiar rattle and swish
of agitate gave her ease.
She looked up to the piping overhead—
copper, no longer lead.
Then her eye caught sight of other eyes,
there in the window!

Beady, golden eyes.
Small staring eyes.
Hungry, jealous eyes.

She screamed.
The washer repeated her fright
with its spin cycle.

The racoon in the window
turned, moved off in the dark,
satisfied.

Between Life and Death

There's a breath.
There's a whisper.
There's an infinitesimal moment
between knowledge
and ignorance—
between life and death.

It's quiet, to many unrecognizable.
It comes as a final release,
an "I give up. I'm tired.
I'm done."
The now says yes,
but the future says no.

Potato-on-a-shoe races for candy prizes,
bottle-drop clothes pins for ribbons,
pin-the-tail provide tales
for forever.

Think now of this knowledge.
It proves.

Who thought, when questioned,
that not knowing the answer
defined ignorance?

Just wait.
The answer may come to you.

Living with the Dead

We don't always stay in the attic
to look out the little square panes
of the tower windows to gaze down the avenue,
see children walk to and from the corner,
watch fathers and mothers ruminate
on their day's work.

No, sometimes we stand behind you
at the dinner table,
especially on Thanksgiving, or Christmas,
when there are other visitors.
We love to hear adults' laughter, children's giggles,
to stare at the crimson of cranberry sauce,
to feel the solid wood of the inherited oak table,
to smell apple pie served with a slice of cheddar.

Sometimes we speak to you,
shout "rise and shine" before the alarm goes off,
voice discovery of your lost briefcase, shoe, math paper,
bellow "have a nice day" as you run out the porch door,
give you the answers to your homework assignments,
tell you a bedtime story that's funny, not scary,
give you clues as to where is that lost recipe
for molasses cookies, shepherd's pie, or babka.

Sometimes we compare our families to yours—
more brothers of sisters, no brother, no sister,
mother, father, grandparents,
aunts, uncles, cousins, wife, husband.
We compare their clothes, their jobs,
how easy or difficult their lives are.
We pat the pets, well, most of them—
the fuzzy dog, the suspicious cat, the dizzy hamster,
the parakeet that loves to fly into the sink's dishwater,
the wiggle-nose rabbit, maybe not the white rat.

We love to enter your dreams
to introduce ourselves, to share our former lives
and our present activities.
We tell tales on each other to you in the night
to let you know who rang the doorbell at 2:00 a.m.,
who let the rat out of its cage,
who hid your favorite, but smelly, pair of socks,
who took the last of your Halloween candy,
put an "I love you" note in your dresser drawer.

For we do love being here.
We wouldn't have it any other way
until we're called,
and you know we are friendly.
We've just always gotten a bad rap.
You'll understand.
We will welcome you.

The Secret

When did you know the secret—
the secret your mother never told,
your father never uttered.
When did you figure it out?

You always thought your sister knew,
or your brother, him being the boy,
and she, being the first born.
You just weren't in the selected order
to be given privy.

The secret was the definition of death.
The secret was don't do what we did.
The secret was keep on keepin' on
as your mother's mother did
after her husband died,
after the depression hit,
after trying to make ends meet on the farm.

The secret is live your own life,
keep safe as you can your children,
your grandchildren.

No one is judging.
No one reaps scale equality.

Joy is a treasure.
Gather it in abundance all your life.
It's not hard to recognize.
Prop up your eyes to see it,
seek it, daily.

You'll need rooms to store it,
rooms with no doors,
perchance to leak the joy
openly to those
who seek it.

www.ingramcontent.com/pod-product-compliance
Lightning Source LLC
Chambersburg PA
CBHW050041080526
44586CB00014B/1410